California
Wine Drinks

William I. Kaufman's

California
Wine Drinks

Cocktails, Coolers,
Punches & Hot Drinks

PUBLISHED BY
THE WINE APPRECIATION GUILD

LIBRARY OF
WINE INSTITUTE

Published by The Wine Appreciation Guild
1377 Ninth Avenue
San Francisco, CA 94122
(415) 566-3532
ISBN 0-932664-19-9

Library of Congress Catalog Card Number

Printed in The United States of America

Cover Design and Illustrations: Bill Lansberg
Contributing Editors: Donna Bottrell
                        Maurice Sullivan
Typography: Vera Allen Composition

Other Books Published by The Wine Appreciation Guild:
EPICUREAN RECIPES OF CALIFORNIA
   WINEMAKERS
THE CHAMPAGNE COOKBOOK
GOURMET WINE COOKING THE EASY WAY
FAVORITE RECIPES OF CALIFORNIA
   WINEMAKERS
NEW ADVENTURES IN WINE COOKERY
WINE COOKBOOK OF DINNER MENUS
EASY RECIPES OF CALIFORNIA WINEMAKERS
THE POCKET ENCYCLOPEDIA OF CALIFORNIA
   WINE
IN CELEBRATION OF WINE AND LIFE
WINE CELLAR RECORD BOOK
WINE IN EVERYDAY COOKING
THE CALIFORNIA WINE DRINK BOOK
THE WINE LOVERS COOKBOOK
CORKSCREWS: An Introduction to Their Appreciation

CONTENTS:

INTRODUCTION

Lest the purist be upset with my idea of a book of wine drinks, let me put their palate at ease with some historical fact.

Wine drinks have a tradition going back 2000 years when the Romans were known to have flavored and spiced their wines. Over the years many non-wine and wine producing countries have added to the Roman beginning. Glogg from Sweden, Negus from England, Kir from France, May Wine from Austria, the Spritzer from Germany, and Sangria from Spain all have a root in the custom of wine-based drinks.

I shudder and go into shock everytime I see someone add champagne to orange juice. But, that is me and if I am to be consistent with my attitude of life and the rights of people, I must say to myself "to each his own." However, when someone wants a Mimosa (usually at Sundy brunch) I serve fresh orange juice and open a $3 bottle of champagne that I have bought and placed in the cooler for that sole purpose.

The drink recipes in this book are the result of many years of drinking wine all over the world, while collecting material for my food and wine books. A wine drink recipe is like a food rec- ipe—to be noted, tried, and then experimented with for the sake of personal taste or personal creative urge. Everybody loves to make little changes in a recipe, a fact that I came to un- derstand while traveling around the country giving my cooking lectures. What I give you here are the ground rules. The most important thing to keep in mind is that making wine drinks, like drinking wine, must be fun.

A wine-based drink can fit any occasion from formal and elegant to informal backyard cook-outs or porch parties, wonderful hot drinks when the frost is on the ground, and ice floating punches for receptions and very special large group parties. Enjoy and have fun with some of my favorite wine drinks.

William I. Kaufman

HOW TO MIX A GOOD WINE DRINK

Glasses

For the serving of wine drinks, the proper glass is recommended not only for esthetic reasons but also for the practical advantages that the proper glass offers. The wrong glass allows the ice to melt quickly and the drink to become warm and diluted. The small glass as opposed to the tall or large allows the drink to stay cool and the drink to remain fresh, cool, and flavorful.

The all-purpose wine glass may be used for cocktails and coolers. However, a regular cocktail glass, champagne coupè, or flute will be more fitting and elegant.

For wine coolers I suggest a not-too-tall highball glass or an old-fashioned glass. The all-purpose wine glass may be easily substituted.

Punches traditionally call for a punch glass or cup. Here again the all-purpose glass may be substituted.

Hot drinks are best served in mugs. If any type glass is used, I suggest using a silver spoon in the glass before pouring in the hot drink.

Chilling & Frosting Glasses

One of the absolute MUSTS for making a good wine drink is the chilling of the glass before mixing the drink. Here are a few suggestions:

1. The simplest way to chill glasses is to place them in the freezer for 10–15 minutes or in the refrigerator for a half-hour.

2. For a large crowd I use a large tub, bucket, or the bathtub full of ice for chilling the wine, and at the same time I scatter the glasses on top of the ice.

3. For an easy frosted glass, dip the glass in water, shake well and place in the freezer.

4. Depending on what your final need is, place sugar, lemon juice, lime juice or wine in a saucer and then dip the rim of the glass in any of the previously mentioned suggestions. Place the glass in the freezer or refrigerator. This is a wonderful touch for the first drink.

Ice

Ice should be used directly from the freezer. Do not use ice that might have been exposed to food odors. Do not skimp on ice and always use fresh ice when fixing the second drink. Keep in mind that the less ice you use, the less diluted the drink becomes. Therefore, if the wine and all other liquid ingredients are well chilled, the less time the liquids being used will be diluted. This especially applies to cocktails.

Fruits, Fruit Juices & Fruit Slices

Use only fresh fruit whenever possible. Peels should be without a trace of white underskin. A paring gadget makes this easy. Fruit juices should be strained. Fruit slices should be cut ¼ inch.

Alcohol Content

"Proof," on a bottle label, is twice the alcohol content by volume. A 90 proof spirit is 45 percent alcohol. The other way around, a wine that is labeled 12 percent (as are most red or white dinner wines, such as Burgundy or sauterne) is 24 proof.

Sweetening

Many hosts use a simple syrup instead of sugar in wine drinks or punches that call for sweetening. They claim it blends faster, tastes smoother. Make syrup by boiling 2 parts sugar and 1 part water for 5 minutes. Keep it handy in a screw-cap bottle in refrigerator and use it to sweeten to taste. Honey will do the same job; it adds, of course, a slight distinctive flavor of its own. Or you can buy rock candy syrup. Or use white corn syrup, but this is less sweet. Dieters can of course use a non-caloric sweetener, available in liquid form as well as tablets, sweetening the drink or punch to taste.

First Wine Glass

The first wine glass is said to have been made from a bubble of seafoam, cut in half by the goddess Aphrodite as she came forth from the sea. Champagne glasses today still have an affinity for saltwater, when it's wash-up time. Saltwater leaves them clean and sparkling. Soap or detergent can leave a faint film that breaks down the champagne bubbles.

CHART OF WINE TYPES

Appetizer Wines

Sherry, Vermouth, and flavored wines.

White Dinner Wines

Sauterne, Sauvignon Blanc, Semillon, Chablis, Chenin Blanc, French Colombard, Pinot Blanc, Pinot Chardonnay, Rhine, Chardonnay, Sylvaner, Riesling, Traminer, Gewurztraminer.

Red Dinner Wines

Burgundy, Gamay, Petite Sirah, Pinot Noir, Chianti, Claret, Cabernet Sauvignon, Merlot, Grignolino, Ruby Cabernet, Zinfandel, Rosé.

Dessert Wines

Muscatel, Angelica, Cream Sherry, Port, Tokay, Botrytis style wines.

Sparkling Wines

Champagne—Natural (very dry), Brut (very dry), Sec (semi-dry), Doux (sweet); Pink Champagne, Sparkling Burgundy, Cold Duck.

TABLE OF MEASURES

California Wine Bottles

3.0 liters	101.0 ounces
1.5 liters	50.7 ounces
1.0 liters	33.8 ounces
750.0 milliliters	25.4 ounces
375.0 milliliters	12.7 ounces
Jeroboam	102.4 ounces
Magnum	51.2 ounces
Quart	32.0 ounces
Fifth	25.6 ounces
Split	6.4 ounces
Miniature	2.0 ounces

Mixing Measurements

1 teaspoon	⅛ ounce
1 tablespoon	½ ounce
2 tablespoons	1 ounce = 1 pony
3 tablespoons	1½ ounces
1 jigger	1½ ounces
¼ cup	2 ounces
⅓ cup	2¾ ounces
½ cup	4 ounces
⅔ cup	5 ounces
¾ cup	6 ounces
1 cup	8 ounces
1 pint	16 ounces
1 quart	32 ounces

Glass Sizes

Tall	10 ounces
Wine Glass	8 ounces
Highball	6 ounces
Old Fashioned	6 ounces
Large Cocktail	6 ounces
Standard Cocktail	4 ounces
Standard	
Champagne	5 ounces
Punch Cup	4 ounces
Average Mug	5 ounces

SERVING CHART

Cups	4-ounce Servings	3-ounce Servings
16	32	42
8	16	21
4	8	11
3⅛	6	8
1½	3	4

Cocktails

FRESNO COCKTAIL

1 pint chilled apple juice
1 cup California dry vermouth
Twist of lemon peel

Stir apple juice and vermouth together; chill thoroughly. Serve with twist of lemon peel in each glass.

Makes about 8 servings.

CARMEL VERMOUTH COCKTAIL

2 cups California dry vermouth
2 teaspoons fresh lime or lemon juice
Ice cubes
5 twists lime or lemon peel
5 stuffed green olives or pearl onions

Measure vermouth and lime juice into cocktail shaker or pint jar. Add ice cubes and stir vigorously until mix is well chilled. Pour into cocktail or all-purpose glasses, adding twist of lime peel and stuffed olive or onion to each glass.

Makes about 5 servings.

Let us drink the juice divine,
The gift of Bacchus, god of wine.

RIVERSIDE APERITIF

2 cups California dry or sweet vermouth
2 teaspoons lime or lemon juice
Ice cubes
5 twists lime or lemon peel

Measure vermouth and lime juice into cocktail shaker or quart jar. Add ice cubes and stir vigorously unitl mix is well chilled. Pour into cocktail or all-purpose glasses adding twist of peel to each glass.

Makes about 5 servings.

SAN FRANCISCO COCKTAIL

⅔ cup California vermouth
⅔ cup California brandy
¼ cups orange juice
½ teaspoon lemon juice
Ice cubes

Place all ingredients in shaker. Shake and chill well. Strain into glasses.

Makes about 4 servings.

BRANDY VERMOUTH COCKTAIL

1 cup California vermouth
½ cup California brandy
Juice of 2 lemons
Ice cubes
Lemon peel

Place all ingredients except lemon peel in shaker. Shake and chill well. Strain into glasses. Garnish with lemon peel.

Makes about 4 servings.

BONNIES'S MARTINI

¼ cup California dry vermouth
⅔ cup California saki
6 ice cubes
Green olives

Place all ingredients except olives in mixing glass. Stir and chill well. Strain into glasses. Add olive to each glass.

Makes about 2 servings.

SARATOGA VERMOUTH CASSIS

½ cup California dry vermouth
2 tablespoons crème de cassis
Club soda
Ice cubes
Lemon peel

Place ice cubes in each glass. Pour in half of vermouth and 1 tablespoon crème de cassis. Add club soda. Garnish with lemon peel.

Makes about 2 servings.

In Vino Veritas

In Wine lies Truth, in Water nought
But Melancholy, dull and sour,
The Apple with old evil's fraught,
The Vine Brings Truth and Friendship's hour!

CHAMPAGNE COCKTAIL

The famous Champagne Cocktail is a favorite of any happy occasion—birthday, christening, wedding, anniversary, going-away party, homecoming, or housewarming. Place ½ teaspoon sugar in champagne glass; add dash of bitters, plus a twist of lemon or orange peel if desired. Fill with well-chilled California champagne; stir lightly.

Frosted glasses are extra glamorous. Pre-chill glass in refrigerator, rub rim with lemon slice, then dip rim into powdered sugar for a few seconds. Shake off excess sugar; proceed with cocktail.

MIMOSA

Use a champagne glass of generous size. Fill it with equal parts of chilled California champagne and freshly squeezed orange juice.

How is Champagne made?
By sheer genius, sheer genius!

--Conversation at White's Club, London

CHAMPAGNE BRANDY COCKTAIL

1 cup California champagne
¼ cup California brandy
¼ teaspoon sugar
¼ teaspoon lemon juice
Dash of bitters
Cracked ice

Combine all ingredients in tall glass. Gently stir. Strain into champagne glasses.

Makes 2 servings.

CHAMPAGNE JULEP

1 (750 ml) bottle California
champagne, chilled
1 cup California brandy
16 sprigs of mint
3 teaspoons sugar
1 tablespoon water
Cracked ice
Mint for garnish

Combine mint sprigs, sugar, and water in a mortar or large cup. Crush together with a muddler. Divide into four glasses. Fill each glass half full with cracked ice. Pour ¼ cup brandy in each glass. Fill glasses with champagne and garnish with mint.

Makes 4 servings.

BO BO'S CHAMPAGNE COCKTAIL

1 (750 ml) bottle California
   champagne, chilled
1 teaspoon orange-flavored liqueur
½ teaspoon bitters
⅓ cup California brandy
Cracked ice
Twists of lemon peel

Combine liqueur, bitters, brandy, and ice in mixing glass. Stir to blend. Strain into glasses. Fill each glass with champagne. Garnish with twist of lemon peel.

Makes 2 servings.

FRENCH 75

1 (750 ml) bottle California
   champagne
Cracked ice
4 teaspoons powdered sugar
4 tablespoons lemon juice
1⅓ cups California brandy

Combine sugar, lemon juice, and brandy in mixing glass. Stir. Fill each glass half full with ice. Pour brandy mixture over ice in each glass. Fill with champagne. Stir gently.

Makes 4 servings.

One barrel of wine can work more miracles than a church full of saints.

JOY'S CHAMPAGNE COCKTAIL

**1 (750 ml) bottle California
  champagne, chilled**
4 sugar cubes
4 dashes of bitters
8 tablespoons California sherry
4 lemon twists
8 ice cubes

Place one sugar cube in each champagne
glass. Add 2 dashes of bitters to sugar.
Add two ice cubes and two tablespoons
of sherry to each glass. Stir gently. Fill
glass with champagne. Garnish with
lemon twist.

Makes 4 servings.

PEACHY IVA

**1 (750 ml) bottle California
  champagne, chilled**
2 fresh peaches, peeled and halved
1 cup California brandy, divided
Fresh mint

Place a peach half in each glass. Using a
fork, pierce each peach many times. Pour
¼ cup brandy over each peach. Fill
glass with champagne. Garnish with fresh
mint.

Makes 4 servings.

Wine is a chemical symphony.

DOCTOR YOUNG SPECIAL

**1 (750 ml) bottle California
champagne, chilled**
¼ cup California brandy
¼ cup pineapple juice
1 cup cracked ice

Place brandy, pineapple juice, and ice in shaker. Shake and chill well. Strain into glasses. Fill each glass with champagne.

Makes about 4 servings.

SHERRIED GRAPEFRUIT COCKTAIL

**1 can (6 oz) frozen grapefruit juice
concentrate**
1½ cups cold water
¾ cup California sherry, chilled

Shake all ingredients together and serve very cold, in prechilled glasses.

Makes about 8 servings.

SHERRY SOUR

4 cups California sherry
**1 can (6 oz) frozen lemonade
concentrate**
Juice of 2 lemons

Mix well with blender or eggbeater. Store 3 to 4 days in refrigerator to blend. Garnish with cherry if desired.

Makes about 10 servings.

SHERRY NOG

2 cups California sherry
½ cup California brandy
¼ cup sugar
4 eggs
Cracked ice
Nutmeg

Place all ingredients except nutmeg in shaker. Shake and chill well. Strain into glasses. Sprinkle with nutmeg.

Makes about 4 servings.

SHERRY MANHATTAN

2 cups California sherry
½ cup California sweet vermouth
¼ teaspoon grenadine
Orange slices

Place sherry, vermouth, and grenadine in bottle with cover. Refrigerate for several hours. Serve chilled. Garnish with orange slices.

Makes about 4 servings.

GRAPEFRUIT SHERRY COCKTAIL

½ cup California sherry
1½ cups grapefruit juice
1 teaspoon sugar
Ice cubes

Place all ingredients in shaker. Shake and chill well. Strain into glasses.

Makes about 4 servings.

VERMOUTH OLD FASHIONED

½ cup California sherry
½ cup California sweet vermouth
4 dashes bitters
Ice cubes
Maraschino cherries

Place all ingredients except cherries in shaker. Shake and chill well. Strain into glasses. Garnish with cherry.

Makes about 2 servings.

PEPPY COCKTAIL

1½ cups California sherry
1 tablespoon sugar
4 eggs
Ice cubes
Paprika

Place all ingredients except paprika in shaker. Shake and chill well. Strain into glasses. Sprinkle with paprika.

Makes about 4 servings.

SHERRY FLIP

1 cup California sherry
1½ cups orange juice
¼ teaspoon salt
2 eggs
1 cup cracked ice
Grated orange rind

Place all ingredients except orange rind in blender. Blend until frothy. Pour into glasses. Sprinkle with grated orange.

Makes about 6 servings.

RIVER CAFE MANHATTAN

½ cup **California sherry**
2 tablespoons **California sweet
  vermouth**
2 tablespoons **California dry
  vermouth**
Ice cubes
Lemon peel

Place all ingredients except lemon peel in shaker. Shake and chill well. Strain into glasses. Garnish with lemon peel.

Makes about 2 servings.

PORT FLIP

½ cup **California port**
2 **eggs**
1 tablespoon **sugar**
⅛ teaspoon **bitters**
Cracked ice
Nutmeg

Place all ingredients except nutmeg in shaker. Shake well to blend and chill. Strain into glasses. Sprinkle with nutmeg.

Makes 2 servings.

STORMY PORT COCKTAIL

½ cup **California port**
¼ cup **California brandy**
1 teaspoon **powdered sugar**
1 **egg**

Place all ingredients in shaker. Shake well to chill and blend. Strain into glasses.

Makes 2 servings.

PERKIN'S PORT COCKTAIL

⅓ cup **California port**
⅓ cup **California brandy**
¼ teaspoon **orange-flavored liqueur**
1 tablespoon **sugar**
2 **egg yolks**
Cracked ice
Nutmeg

Combine all ingredients in shaker. Shake and chill well. Strain into glasses. Garnish with nutmeg.

Makes 2 servings.

CREAMY MUSCATEL COCKTAIL

⅔ cup **California muscatel**
½ cup **California brandy**
2 tablespoons **heavy cream**
1 tablespoon **sugar**
2 **eggs**
1 cup **cracked ice**
Nutmeg

Place all ingredients except nutmeg in blender. Blend for 10-15 seconds. Pour into glasses. Sprinkle with nutmeg.

Makes 4 servings.

He who drinks spirits wants to forget;
He who drinks wine wants to remember.

RED FLIP

1 cup California red dinner wine
Dash of bitters
2 eggs
2 teaspoons sugar
1 cup cracked ice
Nutmeg

Combine all ingredients except nutmeg in blender. Blend at high speed. Pour into glasses and sprinkle with nutmeg.

Makes about 4 servings.

DELLA'S COCKTAIL

½ cup California red dinner wine
⅔ cup California brandy
⅓ cup sugar
⅓ cup lemon juice
Cracked ice

Place all ingredients in shaker. Shake well to mix and chill. Strain into glasses.

Makes 4 servings.

MORTY'S RED COCKTAIL

1 cup California red dinner wine
¼ cup California brandy
1 cup tomato juice
¼ teaspoon Worcestershire sauce
Cracked ice
Lemon slices

Place all ingredients except lemon slices in shaker. Shake and chill well. Strain into glasses. Garnish with lemon slices.

Makes 2 or 4 servings.

EDWARD'S FIZZ

1 cup California white dinner wine
½ cup grapefruit juice
1 teaspoon orange-flavored liqueur
2 teaspoons powdered sugar
2 egg whites
Ice cubes
Club soda, cold

Combine all ingredients except club soda in shaker. Shake well. Strain into glasses. Add cold soda to each glass.

Makes 2 servings.

RENATA'S BLENDER COCKTAIL

1½ cups California white dinner wine
1½ cups cranberry juice
4 tablespoons lemon juice
3 tablespoons honey
Pinch of salt
1 cup crushed ice
2 egg whites

Place all ingredients in blender. Blend at high speed until frothy. Pour into glasses.

Makes 4 servings.

Quickly, bring me a beaker of wine so that I may wet my mind and say something clever.

ORANGE BLOSSOM FLIP

1 (6-oz.) can frozen orange juice
   concentrate
1 cup cream
¾ cup California Sherry
1 egg
Few grains salt
2 ice cubes

Put all ingredients into an electric blender
(or beverage mixer or covered quart jar).
Mix at high speed (or shake vigorously
and thoroughly) until frothy and well
blended. Beverage will about double in
quantity.

(About 1 quart)

KEY TO THE CELLAR

This cocktail has pleasing complexity, and
maintains its aperitif character even
though sweet enough to satisfy the less
sophisticated drinker.

2 tablespoons California Sherry
2 teaspoons triple sec
2 teaspoons California Brandy
2 teaspoons California Dry
   Vermouth
1 teaspoon lemon juice
1 twist orange peel

Shake all liquid ingredients with ice in
cocktail shaker and strain into cocktail
glass. Garnish with orange peel.

(1 serving)

CHANDON JUDY

4 oz Panache
1 oz California Brut Champagne
2–3 drops Angostura Bitters
Lemon Peel

Fill champagne flute, (tall glass) with ice cubes, add the bitters and Panache and top with Champagne. Rub rim of glass with lemon peel and drop in glass, stir gently.

(1 Serving)

CHAMPAGNE A LA SAN FRANCISCO

1 hollow-stemmed Champagne glass
Gin
California Pink Champagne

Chill glass and ingredients. Fill stem of glass with gin. Pour in Champagne until glass is three-fourths full. Serve.

(1 serving)

FRAPPÉ ROSHAR

½ cup California Rhine Wine
½ cup club soda
¼ teaspoon sugar
Juice of 1 slice of lime

Fill a tumbler with crushed ice, add above ingredients, stir well and serve.

(1 serving)

MORNING SHERRY TANG

This is an excellent drink for company brunch and can be prepared with minimum effort.

1 juice glass Tang instant breakfast drink, made with cold water
1-½ ounces California Cream Sherry
Twist of lemon peel

Blend, stir well, and serve "on the rocks", or well chilled from refrigerator.

(1 serving)

GREEN BIRD

Editor's note: This refreshing drink looks as good as it tastes.

1 pint firm lime sherbert
12 ounces California Dry White Wine, well chilled

Combine wine and sherbert in blender at high speed. Mound into chilled glasses and serve with short straws. Sprinkle with nutmeg, if desired.

(8 servings)

GREEN HORNET

½ jigger California brandy
½ jigger melon-flavored liqueur
½ jigger California sake

Pour over ice and strain into a martini glass. Makes 1 drink.

VERMOUTH FROST

For that special person who loves daiquiries, here's a way to make the cold drink with an added flavor of California Dry Vermouth.

¼ cup (2-oz.) California Dry Vermouth
2 tablespoons frozen daiquiri mix
⅓ cup crushed ice

Place all ingredients in blender and blend briefly, about 10 seconds. Serve at once in chilled glass.

(1 serving)

DELMONICO

⅔ jigger gin
⅓ jigger dry vermouth
⅓ jigger sweet vermouth
⅓ jigger California brandy
1 dash angostura bitters
Orange peel

Stir with ice and strain into a cocktail glass. Add orange garnish. Makes 1 drink.

BRONX COCKTAIL

½ oz Panache
½ oz California Dry Vermouth
1 oz Dry Gin

Shake well with ice. Strain into prechilled cocktail glass. Garnish with orange slices.

(1 serving)

BRANDY FINO

1 jigger California brandy
⅓ jigger California dry sherry
⅓ jigger Drambuie
Lemon twist
Orange peel

Stir ingredients with ice and strain into a cocktail glass. Add lemon and orange garnishes. Makes 1 drink.

CLARET COCKTAIL

⅔ jigger dry red wine
⅔ jigger California brandy
½ tablespoon curaçao
½ tablespoon lemon juice
1 dash anisette
Orange peel

Stir with ice and strain into a cocktail glass. Makes 1 drink.

CREAMY ORANGE

⅔ jigger orange juice
⅔ jigger cream sherry
⅓ jigger cream
½ tablespoon California brandy

Shake well with ice and strain into a cocktail glass. Makes 1 drink.

Bronze is the mirror of the form; wine, of the heart.

SHERRY SCREWDRIVER

½ cup orange juice
2 oz California sweet sherry
1 oz Vodka
½ cup crushed ice

Mix all ingredients in blender for 20–30 seconds. Pour over ice cubes in tall glass.

(1 serving)

NAPA DIABLO

1 Jigger Panache
1 Jigger California Dry Vermouth
½ Teaspoon Lemon Juice
Lemon peel

Shake Panache, Vermouth and lemon juice well with ice. Strain into prechilled cocktail glass. Twist lemon peel into drink and drop in glass.

(1 serving)

SIERRA SUNRISE

As an appetizer before breakfast, this prepares one for a day of horseback riding in the mountains.

2 parts orange juice
1 part California Dry Vermouth
1 part California Brandy
1 squeeze lemon

Fill a 10-ounce glass with ice. Add all ingredients. Mix and serve. Serves 1.

SHERRY DAIQUIRI

Sherry Daiquiris have been around for some time under various other names, none of which I can recall.

8 to 10 ice cubes, crushed
1 (6-oz.) can frozen lime juice
1½ (6-oz.) cans California Dry Sherry

Combine crushed ice, lime juice and Sherry in electric blender. Blend and serve immediately.

(About 9 servings, 3-oz. size)

NOTE: *Among the many names for this delectable and popular drink are Sherry Shrub Frappé. Frozen daiquiri mix, limeade or lemonade concentrate are also used—usually 1 (6-oz.) can to 1 (4/5 qt.) bottle of the Sherry.*

NAPA VALLEY DAIQUIRI

1½ oz Panache
Juice of ½ Lime, (freshly squeezed)
1 Teaspoon Sugar

Shake lime juice and sugar with cracked ice, add Panache and shake thoroughly until shaker frosts. Pour into prechilled cocktail glasses.

For a frozen daiquiri: Use shaved ice and mix in blender.

SWEDISH GLOGG

The Swedes have a name for this hot spicy wine drink that warms from head to toes. They call it Julglogg (Christmas Wine). The cardamom should be cracked and tied with the other spices in a little cheesecloth bag. Then it is easy enough to retrieve from the glogg before it is poured into the punch bowl. Stud a few cloves into the orange peel for decorative effect and be sure to serve a little fruit in each glass.

1 (4/5-qt.) bottle California Burgundy
1 (1-qt.) bottle California Port
1 (3-inch) strip orange peel
2 (2-inch) cinnamon sticks
8 whole cardamom, cracked
12 whole cloves
¼ cup sugar
½ cup dark seedless raisins
1 (4-oz.) bottle maraschino cherries
1¼ cups California Brandy
1 cup whole blanched almonds

In large saucepan combine Burgundy and Port with the rest of the ingredients, except ¼ cup Brandy. Heat slowly, just to simmering; pour into punch bowl. Heat remaining Brandy in double boiler; ignite and pour into punch.

(About 20 4-oz. servings)

HOT SPICED (or mulled) wine drinks were quaffed even in Charlemagne's day, as an apéritif. They're one of the oldest of mixed wine drinks known to Northern Europe. And with good reason, you'll know—if you've ever enjoyed a steaming wine bowl on a cold, rainy or snowy night.

HOLIDAY CHOCOLATE

Of course you don't have to wait for any special day to make this delicious hot chocolate, generously laced with California Sherry. Use it for brunch, or depend on its warmth to liven guests some chilly evening on the patio or garden.

½ cup semi-sweet chocolate bits
1 cup California Sherry
Dash of salt
¼ teaspoon cinnamon
3 cups milk
½ cup light cream

In top of double boiler place chocolate bits, Sherry, salt and cinnamon; cook over hot water, stirring occasionally, until chocolate is melted. Heat milk and cream to scalding point; add to Sherry and chocolate mixture and beat well until foamy. Pour into mugs or cups, top with whipped cream (if desired) and dust lightly with cinnamon.
(6 to 8 servings)

> How sweet as through the world we pass,
> to find good folk who love their glass.

CAFÉ BRULOT

This flaming coffee is a version of a very old New Orleans drink. It serves as both dessert and coffee.

15 whole cloves
3 sticks cinnamon, broken in pieces
Peel of ½ orange and ½ lemon, cut in nickel-size pieces
½ cup California brandy
1 tablespoon California Sherry
⅔ cup sugar (or at least 20 cubes)
4 cups hot strong black coffee

Combine spices, peel, brandy, Sherry and sugar; let stand about 4 hours before using. Place in a Brulot bowl, a large Pyrex bowl or a copper-base silver bowl. (Do not use a sterling silver bowl.) Ignite the mixture (during cold weather this works best if mixture is prewarmed before igniting). Stir the flaming liquid with a long-handled spoon or ladle. When flames begin to die down, add piping hot coffee and serve immediately. (To preserve the brandy taste, do not burn too long. Plenty of sugar is required for the rich flavor.)

NOTE: *Some versions of this classic add pieces of vanilla bean. There are also many variations in serving. A favorite one is to light a candle and douse the lights. Heat the spoon or ladle over the candle flame, and with it dip up some of the brandy mixture (not yet flaming) with one or two brandy-soaked lumps of sugar. Touch these off with the candle, then lower the flaming ladle into the bowl to set off the remaining brandy mixture. Add coffee, as above. Great showmanship to climax a special dinner!*

(About 8 demi-tasse cups)

HOT BUTTERED SHERRY

1 (6-oz.) can frozen tangerine juice concentrate
¾ cup California Dry Sherry
2½ cups water
1 Tbs. sugar
¼ tsp. powdered cinnamon
Dash salt
Soft butter
Cinnamon sticks for stirrers

Combine tangerine juice concentrate, Sherry, water, powdered cinnamon and salt. Heat slowly to just below boiling. Pour into mugs and top each serving with a tiny bit of butter. With each mug serve a whole cinnamon stick for a stirrer. Makes 6 servings, 5-oz. size.

SNAPPY TOMATO JUICE

Extremely commendable is this bright and nourishing pick-me-up creation designed for any chilly weather occasion or for a brunch warm up.

2 cups California Dry Sherry
1 (46-oz.) can tomato juice
1 (10½-oz.) can beef bouillon
2 tablespoon each Worcestershire sauce and lemon juice
¼ teaspoon red pepper sauce

Combine all ingredients. Heat slowly to boiling, stirring now and then. Pour into heat-proof glasses or mugs.

(16 4-oz. servings)

HOT CLAM-TOMATO COCKTAIL

A perfect appetizer before a big dinner. To make about 6 servings, 3-oz. size, combine the following: 1 cup tomato juice, 1 (9-oz.) can clam juice, ¼ cup California Dry Vermouth, few drops Tabasco sauce and 2 tablespoons fresh lemon juice. Add salt and pepper to taste. Heat just to boiling and serve in small heat-proof or preheated glasses.

TOMATO JUICE COCKTAIL

The bright good flavor of tomato juice is considerably enlivened with the addition of California Chablis and just a hint of dill. Other white table wines such as California Sauterne or Rhine Wine may be used as a change from the Chablis.

1 cup California Chablis
1 cup tomato juice
¼ teaspoon Worcestershire sauce
Cracked ice
Dried dill
Thin lemon wedges

Measure wine, tomato juice and Worcestershire sauce into shaker; add cracked ice, cover and shake well. Strain into chilled serving glasses. Sprinkle lightly with dill and serve with lemon garnish.

(4 servings)

MONTEREY COCKTAIL

1 cup California white dinner wine
½ cup tomato juice
½ cup clam juice
6 ice cubes
4 lemon slices

Combine all ingredients except lemon slices in shaker. Shake and chill. Strain into glasses. Garnish with lemon slices.

Makes 2 or 4 servings.

BIG SUR

⅔ cup California white dinner wine
⅔ cup California dry vermouth
½ cup California brandy
Ice cubes
Cocktail onions

Place all ingredients except onions in shaker. Shake and chill well. Strain into glasses. Add 1 or 2 cocktail onions to each drink.

Makes 4 servings.

SHERRIED COFFEE DESSERT

In a coffee cup put 1 tablespoon California Sherry, 1 tablespoon California brandy and 3 to 4 tablespoons chocolate ice cream. Fill cup with strong hot coffee and serve at once.

(1 serving)

Coolers

SANGRIA

1 (750 ml) bottle California red
   dinner wine
1 orange
1 lemon or 2 limes, sliced
3 tablespoons California brandy
1 (7 oz) bottle club soda
Variety of fresh fruit (such as 1 or 2
   sliced fresh peaches, 1 or 2 sliced
   plums, and 4 cup fresh berries)
Sugar to taste

Pour wine into glass pitcher. Peel orange
in one long spiral strip. Put peel in wine,
with one end of spiral curled over spout
of pitcher. Squeeze orange; add juice to
wine along with lemon or lime slices and
brandy. For best flavor allow to stand
several hours. One hour before serving,
add remaining fruit. Taste; add sugar, if
desired. (Traditional Sangria is refresh-
ingly fruity but not too sweet.) Just before serving add sparkling water. Pour
Sangria into tall glasses half-filled with ice
cubes. Add fruit to each glass.

Makes about 10 servings.

LAKE COOLER

2 cups California red dinner wine
1 cup lemonade
Cracked ice

Combine wine and lemonade in pitcher.
Fill each glass two-thirds full of cracked
ice. Pour in wine and lemonade.

Makes 4 servings.

SONOMA COOLER

1 (750 ml) bottle California red
   dinner wine
1 tablespoon sugar
1 tablespoon lemon juice
1 tablespoon cherry liqueur
Cracked ice
Marachino cherries

Combine sugar, lemon juice and cherry
liqueur in mixing glass. Fill each glass half
full of cracked ice. Divide lemon juice
mixture into each glass. Fill each glass
with wine. Add cherry.

Makes 4 servings.

TEA REFRESHER

1½ cups California red dinner wine
2 cups double strength tea,
   sweetened
1 cup orange juice
¼ cup lemon juice
Ice cubes
Orange slices

Place all ingredients except ice and
orange slices in pitcher. Stir well. Place
ice cubes in each glass. Pour tea and
wine over ice. Garnish with orange slice.

Makes 6 servings.

German . . .

> There are more old wine drinkers than
> old doctors.

WINE COOLER

A sparkling wine cooler is a favorite refresher anytime. Simply pour half a glass
of your favorite wine red or white. Add 2
or 3 ice cubes and sparkling water or a
fruit-flavored soda to fill. Stir slightly and
serve. Dessert wines, such as port, sherry
or muscatel, as well as the table or dinner
wines, make excellent coolers.

WINE LEMONADE

In a tall glass or large wine glass, mix a
teaspoon or two of sugar with fresh
lemon juice to taste. Fill glass three-
quarters full with shaved or cracked ice.
Pour over ice at least ½ cup red dinner
wine, or sherry, port or muscatel. Fill to
top of glass with water.

Makes 1 tall serving.

EASY WINE COOLER

Just pour half a tall glass (or large wine
glass) of your favorite wine. Drop in a
couple of ice cubes. Add sparkling water
to fill, and stir lightly. Any type of wine
may be used. Most people prefer a
lemon-lime flavored sparkling water.

Makes 1 tall serving.

MAY WINE (MAI BOWLE)

A traditional spring-summer drink you can make ahead, store in refrigerator, and serve in tall wine glasses or a punch bowl. The flavor calls for woodruff (waldmeister), a sweet-scented herb; some pharmacies have it dried. (Or substitute a small bunch of mint and 6 crushed cloves.) Place 1 small bunch of woodruff or substitute in bowl; add (750 ml) bottle white dinner wine; steep 1 hour. Strain out flavorings; add 2 more bottles of the same wine, chilled. Add 2 tablespoons simple syrup or sugar to taste; stir well. Add sugared strawberries if desired.

Makes about 12 tall servings.

APRICOT FROST

2 cups canned apricot nectar
1½ cups California white dinner wine
3 tablespoons fresh lemon juice
¼ cup white corn syrup
1 cup sparkling water
Pineapple or orange sherbet

Chill everything and blend, adding sparkling water just before serving. Top each drink with small scoop of sherbet.

Makes about 6 tall servings.

WHITE WINE SYLLABUB

Combine 4 cups light cream with 1 cup orange juice, grated rinds of 1 orange and 1 lemon, 3 cups white dinner wine and 1 cup sugar. Beat with eggbeater in large bowl until blended; chill well. Pour into tall glasses; top with whipped cream and grated orange rind. Rich, but wonderful. An old favorite since Colonial days.

Makes about 10 tall servings.

FROSTY PINEAPPLE CREAM

1½ cups California white dinner wine
1 pint vanilla ice cream
⅛ teaspoon salt
¼ teaspoon ginger
1 (8½ oz) can crushed pineapple
Chilled club soda or ginger ale

Blend all but sparkling water in blender or with eggbeater. Pour about ½ cup of mixture in each tall glass. Fill with sparkling water or ginger ale; stir gently.

Makes about 6 servings.

By wine we are generous made,
It furnishes fancy with wings;
Without it we ne'er should have had
Philosophers, poets or kings.

SAUTERNE LEMONADE

1 (6 oz) can frozen lemonade
   concentrate
2 cups cold water
1 (750 ml) bottle California white
   dinner wine
Ice cubes
Mint sprigs and lemon slices

Empty can of lemonade concentrate into
large pitcher. Add water, wine, and ice
cubes. Stir to blend. Add fresh lemon
slices, if desired. Garnish with mint sprigs,
more lemon slices, and strawberries or
other fruit in season.

Makes about 8 to 10 servings.

ORANGE FROST

2 cups orange juice
3 tablespoons lemon juice
¼ cup honey
1½ cups California white dinner
   wine
1 cup club soda
Orange sherbet

Combine orange juice, lemon juice,
honey, and wine in a pitcher. Stir. Chill in
refrigerator. Add club soda just before
serving. Pour into glasses and top with
spoonful of sherbet.

Makes 5 servings.

ROSÉ FRUIT FREEZE

1 (750 ml) bottle California rosé
**1 (6 oz) can frozen concentrate for
   raspberry-lemon punch**
1 (6 oz) can water
Juice of 1 lemon

Mix and freeze all ingredients in ice cube trays. Will be "mushy-hard," like a frappé cocktail. Spoon into frosted wine glasses and drink with short straws. Garnish with a raspberry, fresh fruit, or mint.

Makes about 12 servings.

CRANBERRY SHRUB

1 pint bottle cranberry juice cocktail
**1 (6 oz) can frozen pineapple juice
   concentrate**
2 cups California rosé

Combine and pour over ice cubes in large pitcher. Stir to chill.

Makes about 6 servings.

Wine is the most noble and beneficial of alcoholic drinks. Wine is for the sedentary whose work is thinking. Natural wines have been used without drunkenness by millions of human beings for ages. They supply the body with iron, tannin and vitamins.

JACQUIE'S SPARKLE

1 (10 oz) pkg frozen raspberries
¼ teaspoon grated lemon peel
½ cup water
½ cup lemon juice
Pinch of salt
1 (750 ml) bottle California
champagne, well chilled

Bring raspberries, lemon peel and water to boil; lower heat, cover and simmer 10 minutes. Strain through very fine strainer and discard seeds and any pulp left. Stir in lemon juice and salt; chill well. At serving time, stir to blend, then pour several tablespoons into each glass. Fill with champagne; stir gently.

Makes about 5 tall servings.

CHAMPAGNE FIZZ

1 (750 ml) bottle California
champagne, chilled
4 teaspoons sugar, divided
Juice of 4 limes, divided

Place equal amounts of sugar and lime juice in each glass. Fill with champagne.

Makes 4 servings.

Open and free from wiles and arts,
The glow of kindness lights the glass,
Men speak the thing that's in their hearts!

CHAMPAGNE TORPEDO

1 (750 ml) bottle California
   champagne, chilled
1 cup California brandy, divided
4 teaspoons sugar
Bitters
Ice cubes
Lemon peel

Divide brandy, sugar, and a dash of bitters in each glass. Stir. Add ice cubes. Fill with champagne. Garnish with lemon peel.

Makes 4 servings.

PARAMOUNT COOLER

1 (750 ml) bottle California
   champagne, chilled
½ cup California brandy
½ cup California port
1 tablespoon orange-flavored liqueur
⅛ teaspoon bitters
Ice cubes
4 orange slices

Combine brandy, port, liqueur, bitters, and ice cubes in shaker. Shake and chill well. Strain into glasses. Fill with champagne. Garnish with lemon peel.

Makes 4 servings.

ROSIE'S CHAMPAGNE SPRIG

1 (750 ml) bottle California champagne, chilled
4 tablespoons California brandy, divided
4 tablespoons Benedictine, divided
8 ice cubes
4 fresh mint sprigs

Place one tablespoon brandy and one tablespoon Benedictine in each glass. Add two ice cubes to each glass. Fill with champagne. Garnish with sprig of mint.

Makes 4 servings.

SUNDAE FLOAT

1 banana, peeled
1 teaspoon coffee powder
⅛ teaspoon salt
½ cup chocolate sundae sauce
⅓ cup California sherry
1 cup chilled milk
½ pint vanilla ice cream

Blend all in blender at high speed until smooth. (Or mash banana, then beat all with eggbeater or shake well in covered jar.) Serve with cinnamon stick for a stirrer, if desired.

Makes about 4 tall servings.

ORANGE SHERRY FLIP

1 cup California sherry
1½ cups orange juice
2 eggs
¼ teaspoon salt

Have all ingredients well chilled. Shake or whirl in blender until well mixed and frothy. Serve in chilled glasses with mint sprig garnish. For those who like their beverages very cold, mix with ½ cup cracked ice or 6 ice cubes; strain into glasses.

Makes 4 servings.

SHERRIED CHOCOLATE FROST

3½ cups milk
⅔ cup canned chocolate syrup
½ cup California sherry
1 quart vanilla ice cream
Cinnamon

Mix milk, chocolate syrup, and sherry. Place some of the ice cream in each of 6 tall glasses. Pour in chocolate mixture (approximately ¾ cup per glass). Stir briskly and dust with cinnamon. Serve at once, accompanied by straws and iced teaspoons.

Makes 6 servings.

SHERRY-GRAPEFRUIT FIZZ

Mix 1½ cups grapefruit juice, ½ cup
sherry, and 2 egg whites. Stir to blend;
sweeten to taste with powdered sugar.
Add 1 cup cracked ice; shake, beat or
blend vigorously.

Makes 6 servings.

SHERRY SHRUB

4 cups California sherry
1 (6 oz) can frozen lemonade
  concentrate
Juice of 2 lemons

Mix well with blender or eggbeater. Store
3 to 4 days in refrigerator to blend.
Garnish with cherry if desired.

Makes about 10 servings.

SHERRY-GRAPEFRUIT FIZZ

Place ½ cup sherry, 1½ cups grapefruit
juice, and 2 unbeaten egg whites in
shaker or large covered jar. Stir just until
blended; sweeten to taste. Add plenty of
cracked ice and shake madly. Serve in
tall glasses or large wine glasses.

Makes about 4 tall servings.

ZORRI'S FRAPPÉ

⅓ cup California white port
⅓ cup orange juice
2 teaspoons sugar
2 teaspoons lemon juice

Stir to dissolve sugar. Pour over finely crushed ice in tall glass or large wine glass. Serve.

Makes 1 tall serving.

PORTED SODAS

1 (10 oz) package frozen sliced
  strawberries
½ cup bottled strawberry or
  raspberry syrup
2 tablespoons lemon juice
1⅓ cups California port
1½ quarts strawberry or vanilla ice
  cream
Club soda

Combine berries, syrup, lemon juice, and port. When berries are defrosted, stir to blend. Measure 8 cup ported berry syrup into tall soda glasses. Add generous scoop ice cream and stir. Add another scoop of ice cream and fill glass with club soda.

Makes about 8 servings.

A moderate use of wine is the best antidote against alcoholism . . .

PORT AND TONIC

1 cup California port
2 cups quinine water (tonic mixer)
Crushed ice
Lemon wedges for garnish

Pour ¼ cup port and ½ cup quinine water over crushed ice in each of 4 serving glasses. Stir lightly. Garnish with lemon wedges.

Makes 4 servings.

APRICOT-MUSCATEL COOLER

⅓ cup California muscatel
⅓ cup apricot nectar
⅓ cup pineapple juice
1 sprig of mint

Half fill a tall (12 oz) glass with cracked ice. Add muscatel, apricot nectar, and pineapple juice. Stir to blend and chill ingredients. Garnish with mint.

Makes 1 serving.

MARKAY LIMITED

In tall glass or large wine glass, stir ½ cup muscatel with juice of ½ lemon, 2 dashes bitters, 2 squirts of sparkling water, and ice cubes. Fill glass with California white dinner wine.

Makes 1 tall serving.

FRENCH 75 PITCHER

This is a fine, well-tested drink for serving to rather large parties. It's best with a stiff, formal or unhappy crowd!

½ cup California brandy
3 dashes Angostura bitters
3 twists lemon peel
1 large bottle California Demi-sec Champagne, chilled

Fill a large pitcher with ice cubes. Add brandy, bitters and lemon peel (that has first been twisted over ice cubes). Stir; set aside. Just before serving, pour Champagne rapidly over ice cubes. (DO NOT STIR.) Pour into Champagne or cocktail glasses; garnish with orange slices or maraschino cherries. (If a drier Champagne is used, you may want to add about ½ teaspoon sugar.)

(About 10 servings, 3-oz. size)

And how's this for a description of the perfect wine?
"It's like the perfect wife—it looks nice and is nice, natural, wholesome, yet not asertive; gracious and dependable, but never monotonous."

SOPHISTICATED STRAWBERRY SHAKE

1 cup sliced strawberries
⅓ cup sugar
Few grains salt
1 egg
1 cup milk
1 tbs. lemon juice
⅔ cup California Burgundy or other red table wine

Have all ingredients well chilled. Combine strawberries, sugar, salt, egg and milk, and blend in electric blender. Stir in lemon juice and wine, and serve at once. If blender is not available, force strawberries through a sieve, and combine with sugar, salt and egg. Beat until well blended with rotary beater. Stir in milk, then add lemon juice and wine and mix. Serves about 4.

SHERRY BANANA SHAKE

2 large bananas
1 cup milk
1 pint vanilla ice cream
⅛ teaspoon salt
⅓ to ½ cup California Sherry
¼ teaspoon nutmeg

Peel bananas. Combine with all remaining ingredients in electric blender. Blend until smooth and foamy. (If blender is not available, mash banana and beat all ingredients together with a rotary beater until smooth; **or,** shake vigorously in a covered container.)
(2 to 4 servings)

STRAWBERRY SANGRIA

Pink and pretty like an old-fashioned
shrub is this strawberry and wine punch.
Serve it in tall glasses with crushed ice
and garnish with strawberries, lemon and
mint leaves.

2 pints fresh strawberries
1½ cups sugar
3 cups water
1½ cups lemon juice
2 cups California Claret or Rosé

Puree strawberries in electric blender or
force through food mill; sieve to remove
seeds. Combine sugar and water in saucepan, stir and heat slowly until sugar dissolves. Mix with strawberry puree and
lemon juice, then the wine. Chill
thoroughly.
(12 4-oz. servings)

FROSTY ORANGE COOLER

Delightful to serve from its own orange
shell container is this cool and refreshing
drink.

½ cup California Dry Sherry, chilled
½ cup orange juice, chilled
1 tablespoon each honey and lemon
   juice
1 drop mint extract
1 cup crushed ice

Place all ingredients in blender and whirl
to frappé consistency. Fill into orange
shell and garnish with mint leaves. Serve
with straw.
(1 serving)

ICED CRANBERRY ROSÉ

After all ingredients have been chilled and assembled, it's fun to do the drink mixing before your guests. This California Rosé and cranberry juice concoction is easy to make and good to drink.

½ cup California Rosé
2 cups bottled cranberry juice
  cocktail
1 egg white
¼ cup sugar (approximately)

Combine chilled Rosé, cranberry juice cocktail and egg white in cocktail shaker. Stir until well blended, then add sugar to taste. Add a generous amount of cracked ice and shake vigorously. Strain into chilled Champagne or cocktail glasses.

(6 servings)

PANACHE COOLER

3 oz. Panache
Club Soda
Lemon twist or lime slice

Pour Panache into tall glass filled with ice cubes, top up with soda and garnish with the lemon or lime.
For a sweeter drink, use ginger-ale or lemon-lime soda.

They who have loved good wine grow never old.

WINE SNOW CONES

Bowl of shaved or crushed ice
Assortment of full-bodied California
**   wines**
Straws

Inspired by children's snow cones, these
are for adults. Fill each guest's glass
nearly to the brim with ice. Let each
guest pour the wine of his choice over
the ice (about 3 oz.). Insert straw and sip,
or serve with a spoon and nibble, for a
wine-flavored ice cooler. Easy and
refreshing.

NOTE: *Offering a choice of several California wine
types adds special interest for guests, and extra
color.*

PEACHES AND WINE COOLER

Something quite different, cool and
temptingly flavored, this drink would be
especially pleasant some warm afternoon.

1 (10½-oz.) package frozen peaches,
**   partially thawed**
3 or 4 drops almond extract
1 tablespoon lemon juice
1 (4/5-qt.) bottle California Chablis
**   Nutmeg**

Whirl peaches, almond extract, lemon
juice and half the wine in blender until
smooth. Stir in remaining wine. Pour into
chilled glasses and fleck with nutmeg.

(5 to 6 servings)

AFTER-DINNER PEACHIE

4 small (half-dollar size) ripe peaches, peeled
¾ cup California brandy
1 tablespoon powdered sugar
1 large bottle California Sec or Brut Champagne, chilled

Pierce peeled peaches thoroughly with a fork. Place in small glass bowl. Pour over brandy; sprinkle with powdered sugar. Refrigerate overnight. When ready to serve, place each peach in a tall, clear, zombie-type glass. Gently pour Champagne over peach, filling glass ⅔ full. If peach is small enough to move in glass, the effervescence of the Champagne will cause the peach to swirl.

NOTE: *This is a traditional combination serving as both dessert and after-dinner drink. It is also attractive served in a regular wine glass or a Champagne glass. Guests eat the peach with a spoon, then drink the Champagne.*

(4 generous servings)

SHERRIED SPICED TEA

The little tea bag makes it easy to make a cup of good relaxing tea. Add California Sherry and spices to make it even better. Rinse mug or glass with hot water. Pour about ⅓ cup boiling water over tea bag and let stand about a minute. Remove tea bag, add ⅓ cup California Dry or Medium Sherry, a dash of nutmeg and cinnamon.

APRICOT PICTHER PUNCH

One of the best thirst-quenchers ever stirred together in a large pitcher is this combination of California Sauterne and apricot nectar. It looks cool and delicate and tastes delightful. Instead of Sauterne you might use Chablis or Riesling.

1 (4/5-qt.) bottle California Sauterne or other white table wine, chilled
2 (12-oz.) cans apricot nectar, chilled
¼ cup lemon juice
½ cup sugar
1 (1-qt.) bottle gingerale, chilled

In large pitcher combine Sauterne, apricot nectar, lemon juice and sugar; stir until sugar is dissolved. Chill pitcher and contents. Just before serving, pour in gingerale. Pour over ice cubes in tall glasses.

(About 12 6-oz. servings)

VERMOUTH CASSIS

A favorite continental refresher (if your dealer carriers crème de cassis or black currant liqueur). Put ¼ cup of dry vermouth in a large wine glass, with 1 tablespoon crème de cassis. Stir, with ice cubes. Add sparkling water to fill. (A teaspoon or two of the cassis stirred into chilled white dinner wine is another dandy).

BURGUNDY REFRESHER

Another quick but easy to make drink is this California Burgundy and fruit juice combination with excellent color and flavor.

Crushed ice
2 cups California Burgundy
2 cups cranberry-apple drink
Mint sprigs for garnish

Fill glasses half full with crushed ice. Add Burgundy and cranberry-apple drink in equal parts (½ cup each) in each glass. Stir gently. Garnish glasses with sprigs of mint.

(4 servings)

SPARKLING BURGUNDY CUP

1½ cups water
3 whole sticks cinnamon
6 whole cloves
½ teaspoon ground nutmeg
4 thin lemon slices
3 tablespoons sugar
1 large bottle California Sparkling
Burgundy, well chilled

First make spice syrup as follows: Boil water, spices, lemon slices and sugar together in covered saucepan about 10 minutes. Strain through very fine strainer; discard spices and lemon; chill liquid thoroughly. When ready to serve, pour about 1 tablespoon (or more, to taste) of spice syrup into each cup. Fill with Sparkling Burgundy. (Leftover syrup can be stored in refrigerator.)

(About 8 servings, 3-oz. size)

SHERRIED TEA FLIP

A well chilled drink that is made frothy by beating ice cream and California Sherry into it. There's a whisper of spice too.

¼ cup instant tea
¼ cup sugar
⅛ teaspoon cinnamon
Dash mace
3 cups cold tap water
1 pint vanilla ice cream, softened
¾ cup California Cream Sherry

Combine instant tea, sugar and spices; add cold water and stir briskly. Beat in ice cream and Sherry until smooth and frothy. Pour into tall glasses and serve.

(4 servings)

TOMATO VERMOUTH

2 cups chilled tomato juice
1 cup California dry vermouth
2 tablespoons fresh lemon juice

Combine ingredients. Shake well and chill before serving.

Makes about 8 servings.

The proper tempo for wine drinking is leisurely. It is almost meditative. It aids in digestion, supplies needed vitamins and carbohydrates and suffuses the whole being with a warmth and friendliness not to be captured by any other means.

Punches

A spectacular punch bowl for summer is a scalloped watermelon shell. Slice off top of melon. Cut around inside edge and make three cross-cuts, lifting out melon in chunks. (Refrigerate chunks, for use later). Remove seeds in bottom; scrape with spoon to smooth. Cut scalloped paper pattern. Outline scallops at top edge of melon with small knife point; then cut along outline. Chill melon shell thoroughly before pouring in punch.

Large blocks of ice in your punch bowl dilute the punch less than ice cubes. To save time, make your own blocks. Just freeze in ice trays without cube dividers. You can still add color to these larger ice blocks by using fruit juice instead of water, or by freezing fruit or flowers in the liquid. It's fun to experiment.

Try making the punch bowl itself from a huge block of ice, to dazzle guests. Select block size according to amount of punch it must hold. (Ice blocks are usually 25, 50, 100, 200 or 300 pounds). If ice has been stored at zero degrees, let it stand at room temperature about 20 minutes before you start shaping the bowl. Start hole in top center of block by chipping lightly with chisel. Chip carefully; ice is brittle and can split if hit too hard. Place metal pan in hole and keep pan filled with very hot water until depression is desired size. Corners can be rounded by scraping. When serving, set ice on tray or shallow pan to take care of melting. Conceal pan with leaves or flowers.

MT. VEEDER SPECIAL

1 (750 ml) bottle California Champagne, chilled
2 (750 ml) bottles California white dinner wine, chilled
¼ cup California brandy
1 tablespoon cherry brandy
¼ cup Benedictine
¼ cup Chartreuse
¼ cup orange-flavored liqueur
Ice block

Place ice block in punch bowl. Pour brandies and liqueurs into punch bowl. Stir. Add wine. Stir. Add Champagne. Stir gently. Serve.

Makes about 30 servings.

APPLE CHAMPAGNE PUNCH

2 (750 ml) bottles California Champagne, chilled
2 quarts apple juice, chilled
⅓ cup lemon juice
4 cups pineapple chunks, drained
1 cup maraschino cherries, drained
Grapes
Ice block

Place ice in punch bowl. Pour champagne, apple juice, and lemon juice into punch bowl. Stir gently. Add fruits. Stir gently. Serve and ladle fruit with punch into glasses.

Makes about 40 servings.

PEACH MAY WINE

1 (750 ml) bottle California
  Champagne, chilled
1 (750 ml) bottle California white
  dinner wine, chilled
1 cup peach brandy, chilled
Fresh peach slices

Pour champagne, wine, and brandy in
large pitcher. Stir gently. Place a few
peach slices in each punch glass. Serve.

Makes about 16 servings.

CHERRY DUCK PUNCH

2 (750 ml) bottles California cold
  duck, chilled
2 (750 ml) bottles California
  Champagne, chilled
1 cup port
1 cup cherry brandy or liqueur
Juice of 3 lemons
Juice of 3 oranges
Ice block
Fresh peach slices

Place ice block in punch bowl. Pour all
ingredients except peach slices over ice.
Stir gently. Add peach slices. Serve.

Makes about 40 servings.

French . . .

> In water one sees one's own face, but in
> wine one beholds the heart of another.

GARDEN PUNCH

**4 (750 ml) bottles California pink
  Champagne, chilled**
**2 (750 ml) bottles California rosé
  wine, chilled**
**4 (6 oz) cans frozen pink lemonade
  concentrate, thawed**
1 cup sugar
6 cups strawberries, fresh or frozen
Ice block
Orange and lemon slices

Combine rosé, lemonade concentrate,
sugar, and strawberries in punch bowl.
Stir until sugar is dissolved. Add ice. Add
strawberries. Stir. Pour in champagne.
Stir gently. Garnish with fruit slices.
Serve.

Makes about 50 servings.

MISSION PUNCH

**2 (750 ml) bottles California pink
  Champagne, chilled**
**2 (750 ml) bottles California white
  dinner wine, chilled**
1 cup California brandy
1 (1 qt) bottle club soda
½ cup lemon juice
Ice block
Orange slices

Place ice in punch bowl. Pour all ingredients over ice. Stir gently. Garnish with
orange slices. Serve.

Makes about 40 servings.

PINK PANTHER PUNCH

2 (750 ml) bottles California pink
   Champagne, chilled
1 (1 qt) bottle club soda, chilled
1 cup California white dinner wine
1 quart raspberry sherbet, softened
½ cup cherry-flavored liqueur
1 (6 oz) can frozen pink lemonade
   concentrate, thawed
2 cups raspberries, fresh or frozen
Ice block
Fresh mint

Combine wine, sherbet, liqueur, and lemonade concentrate in punch bowl. Stir.
Add ice. Add raspberries and club soda.
Stir gently. Pour in champagne. Stir
gently. Pour into punch cups and garnish
with fresh mint. Serve.

Makes about 38 servings.

JACQUELINE'S TEA PUNCH

2 (750 ml) bottles California
   Champagne, chilled
⅓ cup California brandy
¼ cup orange-flavored liqueur
1 teaspoon sugar
¼ cup lemon juice
2 cups double strength tea, cold
Ice block

Combine brandy, liqueur, sugar, lemon
juice, and tea in punch bowl. Stir. Add
ice. Pour in champagne. Stir gently.
Serve.

Makes about 22 servings.

PEACH PUNCH

**3 (750 ml) bottles California
    Champagne, chilled**
2 cups California brandy, chilled
2 tablespoons sugar
**4 cups sliced fresh or frozen
    peaches**
Ice block

Combine brandy, sugar, and peaches in
punch bowl. Stir. Add ice. Pour in champagne. Stir gently. Serve.

Makes about 30 servings.

ST. HELENA CHAMPAGNE PUNCH

**1 (750 ml) bottle California
    Champagne, chilled**
**2 cups California white dinner wine,
    chilled**
½ cup lemon juice
1 cup sugar
4 oranges, sliced
Ice block

Combine wine, lemon juice, and sugar in
punch bowl. Stir until sugar is dissolved.
Add ice. Pour in champagne. Stir gently.
Garnish with orange slices. Serve.

Makes about 14 servings.

Irish . . .

> Take the drink for the thirst that is yet to
> come.

IVA'S PARTY PUNCH

1 (750 ml) bottle California Champagne, chilled
1 (750 ml) bottle California sweet white dessert wine, chilled
1 cup sugar
¼ teaspoon powdered ginger
½ cup grapefruit juice
3 cups unsweetened pineapple juice, chilled
1 cup orange juice, chilled
½ cup lemon juice
1 cup double strength cold tea
Grapes
Ice block

Combine wine, sugar, ginger, fruit juices, and tea in punch bowl. Stir until sugar is dissolved. Add ice. Stir. Pour in champagne. Stir gently. Garnish with grapes. Serve.

Makes about 30 servings.

CHAMPAGNE FRUIT PUNCH

1 (750 ml) bottle California Champagne, chilled
1 (750 ml) bottle California white dinner wine, chilled
½ cup California brandy
½ cup pineapple juice
¼ cup lemon juice
¼ cup orange juice
Ice block

Place ice in punch bowl. Add all ingredients except champagne. Stir. Add champagne. Stir gently. Serve.

Makes about 20 servings.

DONNA'S PUNCH BOWL

2 (750 ml) bottles California
    Champagne, chilled
1 (750 ml) bottle California cold
    duck, chilled
½ cup California brandy
1 cup sugar
1 (1 qt) bottle club soda, chilled
Orange slices
Ice block

Combine brandy and sugar in punch
bowl. Stir until sugar is dissolved. Add
ice. Pour in champagne, cold duck, and
club soda. Stir gently. Garnish with orange slices. Serve.

Makes about 32 servings.

LUBA'S PUNCH

2 (750 ml) bottles California
    Champagne, chilled
1 cup California brandy
2 cups California sherry, chilled
2 cups California port, chilled
½ cup sugar
2 (1 qt) bottles ginger ale, chilled
Ice block
Orange and lemon slices

Combine brandy, sherry, sugar, and port
in punch bowl. Stir until sugar is
dissolved. Add ice. Pour in ginger ale and
champagne. Stir gently. Garnish with
fruit slices.

Makes about 44 servings.

SANTA CRUZ SPECIAL

2 (750 ml) bottles California Champagne, chilled
2 (750 ml) bottles California white dinner wine, chilled
2 cups California sherry, chilled
4 cups canned crushed pineapple, drained
2 cups lemon juice, chilled
2 (16 oz) packages frozen raspberries, thawed
Ice block

Place ice block in punch bowl. Add all ingredients except champagne to punch bowl. Stir. Add champagne. Stir gently. Serve.

Makes about 40 servings.

CHAMPAGNE RASPBERRY PUNCH

2 (750 ml) bottles California Champagne, chilled
1 cup California white dinner wine
4 cups raspberries
2 tablespoons lemon juice
Ice block

Combine wine, raspberries, and lemon juice in separate bowl. Stir. Place ice in punch bowl. Add raspberry mixture. Pour champagne over ice. Stir gently.

Makes about 24 servings.

PARTY CHAMPAGNE PUNCH

2 cups sliced fresh or frozen
  peaches
2 cups melon balls
2 cups halved fresh strawberries
¼ cup sugar
1 tablespoon lemon juice
2 (750 ml) bottles California white
  dinner wine
2 (750 ml) bottles California
  Champagne

Combine fruits, sugar, lemon juice, and
wine. Refrigerate several hours. Pour into
chilled punch bowl over a small block
of ice. Add chilled champagne.

Makes about 30 servings.

SACRAMENTO PUNCH

1 (750 ml) bottle California
  Champagne
½ cup sugar
1 cup fresh lemon juice
2 cups apple juice
2 cups orange juice

Chill champagne at least 4 hours. Combine other ingredients; stir until sugar is
dissolved. Chill well. Just before serving
add champagne.

Makes about 20 servings.

Wine improves with age—I like it more the
older I get.

CHAMPAGNE PUNCH

2 lemons
4 oranges
1 can (No. 2) pitted dark sweet
  cherries
1 (750 ml) bottle California white
  dinner wine
½ cup brandy
Ice
1 (750 ml) bottle California
  Champagne, chilled
Long spirals of orange peel
Long spirals of lemon peel

Cut peel from lemons and oranges in
long spirals; squeeze juice from fruit.
Combine with undrained cherries, wine,
and brandy. Cover and refrigerate overnight. Pour over ice in punch bowl. Add
champagne just before serving. Garnish
with freshly cut spirals of orange and
lemon peel, if desired. If sweeter punch is
preferred, stir in white corn syrup or bar
sugar to taste.

Makes about 20 servings.

SPARKLE PUNCH

2 (750 ml) bottles California
  sparkling Burgundy, chilled
1 (1 qt) bottle club soda
½ cup brandy
½ cup orange-flavored liqueur
Ice block

Place ice in punch bowl. Pour in all ingredients. Stir gently. Serve.

Makes about 26 servings.

CHAMPAGNE ORANGE PUNCH

**2 (6 oz) cans frozen orange juice
concentrate**
**1 (6 oz) can frozen lemonade
concentrate**
14 quarts ice water
**1 (750 ml) bottle California
Champagne**
Orange slices

Dilute orange juice and lemonade concentrates with ice water in punch bowl. Just before serving add well-chilled champagne and garnish with orange slices.

Makes about 30 servings.

CHAMPAGNE PEACH PUNCH

2 (12 oz) cans peach nectar
**1 (6 oz) can frozen orange juice
concentrate**
3 cups water
2 cup lemon juice
1/8 teaspoon salt
**3 (750 ml) bottles California
Champagne, well chilled**

Combine all ingredients except champagne and chill well. At serving time put in punch bowl over small chunk of ice or ice cubes. Add chilled champagne.

Makes about 42 servings.

A WEDDING PUNCH

6 oranges
6 lemons
4 cups sugar
2 cups water
½ cup white corn syrup
¼ teaspoon salt
2 quarts pineapple or orange juice
(or mixed half-and-half)
2 cups lemon juice
2 (750 ml) bottles California white
dinner wine
2 (750 ml) bottles California
Champagne
2 large bottles sparkling water

Peel oranges and lemons. Cut peel in thin strips; add sugar, water, syrup, and salt. Bring to boil, stirring to dissolve sugar. Lower heat; simmer 15 minutes. Cover and cool; remove peel. Add cold syrup mixture to fruit juices and white dinner wine; pour over block of ice in large punch bowl. Let stand about one-half hour, stirring once or twice. Add candied peel strips if desired. Add well-chilled champagne and sparkling water before serving.

Makes about 80 servings.

As the nightingale from rose-tree sips,
Wise it is, and knows that it is good;
Thus with wine we damp our rosy lips,
Wise are we and know that it is good.

MARQUEZ CHAMPAGNE PUNCH

1 (750 ml) bottle California Champagne
1 (13½ oz) can frozen pineapple chunks
½ cup sugar
⅔ cup fresh lemon juice
¼ cup syrup from maraschino cherries

Combine all ingredients except champagne and let stand in refrigerator until pineapple is thawed. Just before serving add well-chilled champagne. Mix lightly and serve immediately.

Makes about 15 servings.

RED PUNCH

1 (750 ml) bottle California sparkling Burgundy, chilled
⅔ cup California white dinner wine
6 whole cloves
2 cinnamon sticks
Peel of 1 lemon
½ cup sugar
2 cups orange juice, chilled
1 cup pineapple juice, chilled
½ cup lemon juice
Ice block

Place white wine, cloves, cinnamon, lemon, and sugar in saucepan. Boil for 10 minutes. Strain. Cool. Place ice in punch bowl. Pour in spice mixture, burgundy, and juices. Stir gently. Serve.

Makes about 18 servings.

STRAWBERRY PUNCH

**2 (750 ml) bottles California
    sparkling Burgundy, chilled**
2 (1 qt) bottles club soda, chilled
½ cup lemon juice
Ice block
Fresh strawberries

Place ice block in punch bowl. Pour in
burgundy, club soda, and lemon juice.
Stir gently. Place strawberry in each
punch glass. Serve.

Makes about 32 servings.

AMADOR PUNCH

**1 (750 ml) bottle California
    sparkling Burgundy, chilled**
**2 cups California red dinnner wine,
    chilled**
1 cup brandy
2 tablespoons sugar
2 cups club soda, chilled
Grapes
Ice block

Combine red wine, brandy and sugar in
punch bowl. Stir until sugar is dissolved.
Add ice. Pour club soda and burgundy
over ice. Stir gently. Serve.

Makes about 20 servings.

With wine and hope, anything is possible.

SPARKLING FRUIT PUNCH

**1 (750 ml) bottle California
   sparkling Burgundy, chilled**
1½ cups club soda, cold
¼ cup California brandy
Cucumber slices
Orange slices
Rind of 1 lemon, cut in strips
Rind of 1 orange, cut in strips
Cracked ice

Place all ingredients except burgundy in
large pitcher. Stir. Add burgundy and stir
gently. Serve.

Makes about 10 servings.

SPARKLING BURGUNDY BOWL

1 (46 oz) can grapefruit juice
**2 (10 oz) packages frozen
   raspberries**
¼ cup lemon juice
½ cup sugar
⅛ teaspoon salt
**3 (750 ml) bottles California
   sparkling Burgundy, well chilled**

Combine all ingredients except wine and
stir until sugar is dissolved, and raspberries are slightly thawed. Put in punch
bowl over small chunk of ice or ice
cubes. When ready to serve, add sparkling burgundy. A colorful punch, and full
of flavor.

Makes about 40 servings.

YOUNTVILLE PUNCH

**1 (750 ml) bottle California cold
duck, chilled**
**1 (750 ml) bottle California white
dinner wine, chilled**
½ cup sugar
Peel of 3 lemons, cut in strips
Lemon slices from 3 peeled lemons
Juice of 1 lemon

Place lemon peel, juice, slices, and sugar
in large pitcher. Pour in wines. Cover
with foil or plastic wrap. Place in refrigerator and chill. Stir occasionally. Serve
when well chilled.

Makes about 16 servings.

CALISTOGA PUNCH

**1 (750 ml) bottle California cold
duck, chilled**
½ cup California sherry, chilled
**1 (6 oz) can frozen lemonade
concentrate, thawed**
Orange slice
Ice cubes

Pour cold duck, sherry, and lemonade
concentrate into large pitcher. Stir. Add
orange slices. Place ice cube in each cup.
Pour and serve.

Makes about 10 servings.

Old wine and old friends are enough
provision.

DUCK BOWL

1 (750 ml) bottle California cold
   duck, chilled
12 whole cloves
2 cinnamon sticks
Peel of 1 lemon
½ cup sugar
¾ cup water
½ cup lemon juice
1 cup pineapple juice
1 cup orange juice
2 cups club soda
Ice block
Orange and lemon slices

Place cinnamon, lemon peel, sugar, and
water in saucepan. Boil for five minutes.
Cool and strain. Place ice in punch bowl.
Pour in spice mixture and fruit juices.
Stir. Pour in cold duck and club soda.
Stir. Garnish with orange and lemon
slices. Serve.

Makes about 20 servings.

COLD DUCK CUP

1 (750 ml) bottle California cold
   duck, chilled
¼ cup California brandy
¼ cup blackberry brandy
Orange, lemon, and pineapple slices
Cracked ice

Half fill a large pitcher with cracked ice.
Add brandies and fruit slices. Stir. Add
cold duck. Stir. Serve.

Makes about 10 servings.

PINEAPPLE PUNCH

1 (750 ml) bottle California red dinner wine
¼ cup California brandy
3 tablespoons sugar
3 tablespoons orange-flavored liqueur
1 tablespoon blackberry brandy
4 slices canned pineapple, drained
1 orange sliced in rounds
1 lemon sliced in rounds
Ice cubes
1 cup club soda

Combine all ingredients except club soda in large pitcher. Stir. Add club soda. Serve.

Makes about 10 servings.

BABES PUNCH

2 (750 ml) bottles California red dinner wine, chilled
½ cup California sherry, chilled
½ cup California brandy, chilled
¼ cup orange-flavored liqueur
½ cup sugar
Rind of 1 lemon, cut in strips
Ice block
2 (1 qt) bottles club soda, chilled

Combine wine, sugar, and lemon rind in punch bowl. Mix well until sugar is dissolved. Add ice block. Add sherry, brandy, and liqueur. Stir. Add club soda just before serving.

Makes about 40 servings.

WINTER PUNCH

1 (750 ml) bottle California red
   dinner wine
2 cinnamon sticks
12 whole cloves
1 whole lemon rind
1/3 cup sugar
3/4 cup California white dinner wine
1 cup syrup from canned sliced
   peaches
3/4 cup lemon juice
3/4 cup orange juice
2 cups club soda
Lemon and orange slices
Canned peach slices, drained—
   reserve juice
Ice block

Place cinnamon sticks, cloves, lemon
rind, and sugar in saucepan and boil for
five minutes. Set aside and cool. Strain
into punch bowl. Place ice block in
punch bowl. Add remaining ingredients.
Stir. Garnish bowl with orange, lemon,
and peach slices.

Makes about 20 servings.

SHERBET-WINE PUNCH

For a quick, frothy punch, as thick as a
milkshake, combine 1 quart pineapple
sherbet with 1 (750 ml) bottle white dinner wine. Stir until smooth.

Makes about 12 servings.

CRANBERRY WINE PUNCH

1 pound cranberries
1 quart boiling water
2 cups sugar
1 (750 ml) bottle California red dinner wine, chilled
1 (6 oz) can frozen orange juice concentrate
½ cup lemon juice
1 large bottle club soda, chilled

Cook cranberries in boiling water until skins pop; strain through fine sieve. Add sugar; stir over low heat to dissolve. Chill. At serving time, mix cranberry juice, wine, orange juice concentrate, and lemon juice in punch bowl. Add large block of ice and sparkling water; stir well. (Also good as a wine cooler over ice cubes in tall glasses.)

Makes about 30 servings.

LODI WINE APPLE PUNCH

2 (750 ml) bottles California red dinner wine
1 quart bottle apple juice, chilled
2 tablespoons lemon juice
1 cup sugar
1 large bottle ginger ale, chilled

Combine wine, apple juice, lemon juice, and sugar in punch bowl; stir to dissolve sugar. Blend in ginger ale. Add block of ice or tray of ice cubes. Serve at once.

Makes about 35 servings.

SPICED WINE PUNCH

24 whole cloves
24 whole allspice
1 tablespoon broken cinnamon
 sticks
1 medium-sized ginger root
1 cup sugar
2 cups water
1 (6 oz) can frozen lemonade
 concentrate, undiluted
1 (48 oz) can unsweetened
 pineapple juice, chilled
2 (750 ml) bottles California red
 dinner wine, chilled
1 large bottle club soda, chilled

Combine spices, sugar, and water; boil
15 minutes. Cool and strain. In a punch
bowl mix spiced syrup and frozen lemonade concentrate. Stir in pineapple juice
and wine. Add block of ice. Just before
serving, add sparkling water. Attractive
garnish: clove-studded orange slices.

Makes about 50 servings.

SHERRY DELIGHT PUNCH

1 (750 ml) bottle California white
 dinner wine, chilled
½ cup California sherry
1 cup peach slices, drained
1 (1 qt) bottle club soda
Ice block
Lemon slices

Place ice in punch bowl. Pour wines over
ice. Stir. Add peaches. Stir. Add club
soda. Garnish with lemon slices.

Makes about 20 servings.

WHITE WINE SYLLABUB

**1 (750 ml) bottle California white
  dinner wine, chilled**
⅓ cup lemon juice
¼ cup grated lemon rind
1 cup sugar, divided
2 cups light cream
3 cups cold milk
4 egg whites
Nutmeg

Combine wine, lemon juice, lemon rind,
and one half cup sugar in punch bowl.
Stir until sugar is dissolved. Add cream
and milk. Whip until foamy. In separate
bowl beat egg whites and half cup sugar
until meringue forms. Add dollops of
meringue to top of punch. Sprinkle with
nutmeg.

Makes about 20 servings.

DRY CREEK PUNCH

**1 (6 oz) can frozen lemonade
  concentrate**
1 (46 oz) can pineapple juice
**2 (750 ml) bottles California white
  dinner wine**
**1 (750 ml) bottle California
  Champagne**
**Orange slices, maraschino cherries,
  or strawberries for garnish**

Combine frozen lemonade concentrate
and chilled pineapple juice in punch
bowl. Add chilled wine. Mix well. Add
one tray of ice cubes. Just before serving
pour in cold champagne.

Makes about 45 servings.

WINDSOR PICNIC PUNCH

2 (750 ml) bottles California white
   dinner wine
2 (6 oz) cans frozen pineapple-
   grapefruit juice concentrate
1 (6 oz) can frozen orange juice
   concentrate
Ice

Pour wine and fruit juice concentrates
into a gallon thermos jug or insulated
container. Fill container with ice cubes.
Cover tightly and carry along to picnic or
other outing. Punch will be mixed, prop-
erly diluted, and chilled when ready to
drink.

Makes about 20 servings.

MAY WINE

1 small bunch mint
1 teaspoon crushed cloves
3 (750 ml) bottles California white
   dinner wine
2 cups halved strawberries, if
   desired
Ice
Spring flowers (violets, daisies, etc.)

Place small bunch of mint leaves and
crushed cloves in punch bowl. Add 1
bottle wine. Set aside for one hour. Chill
remaining wine. Remove flavorings; pour
in remaining 2 bottles of wine. Stir well.
Add strawberries. Add ice just before
serving and float spring flowers on the
top of punch.

Makes about 25 to 30 servings.

SOLVANG PARTY PUNCH

2 (16 oz) packages frozen strawberries
½ cup sugar
Few grains salt
⅔ cup port
4 lime or lemon slices
1 mint sprig (½ teaspoon dried mint)
2 (750 ml) bottles California white dinner wine, chilled

Combine strawberries, sugar, salt, port, citrus slices and mint; bring to boil. Lower heat; simmer 10–15 minutes. Cool, strain and chill well. Blend strawberry syrup with chilled white wine. Add ice to punch bowl, if desired. Garnish with thin lime slices or mint sprigs.

Makes about 21 servings.

SANTA MARIA PUNCH

1 (750 ml) bottle California white dinner wine, chilled
1 quart lemon-flavored sparkling beverage (such as "collins" mix, lemon-lime soda, etc), chilled

Combine just before serving. They don't come much easier, or more colorful, garnished with mint, lemon slices, or cocktail cherries. Nice over ice cubes in tall glasses, too.

Makes about 18 servings.

APRICOT MINTED PUNCH

1 (750 ml) bottle California white dinner wine
1 (7 oz) bottle club soda
1 tablespoon chopped fresh mint (or dried mint)
3 tablespoons fresh lemon juice
1/3 cup orange juice
1/3 cup sugar
1 (12 oz) can apricot nectar

Chill wine and sparkling water 4 hours. Stir mint, lemon juice, orange juice, and sugar until mint is well bruised and sugar dissolved. Add nectar; chill 1 hour. Strain. Pour chilled wine and nectar over ice block in chilled punch bowl. Add sparkling water. Garnish with fresh strawberries and mint sprigs, as desired.

Makes about 15 servings.

SHERRY-APPLE PUNCH

4 cups chilled apple cider or apple juice
1 cup California sherry
1/4 cup lemon juice

Combine and chill well.

Makes about 14 servings.

Sunbeams condensed from Nature's Holy Shrine
Are gently housed in every drop of wine.

LUCILLE'S FRUIT PUNCH

**1 (6 oz) can frozen pineapple-
grapefruit juice concentrate**
**1 (6 oz) can frozen orange juice
concentrate**
**1 (6 oz) can frozen lemonade or
limeade concentrate**
1 quart cold water
4 cups California sherry
1 quart club soda or ginger ale

Combine undiluted frozen juice concentrates with water and sherry; chill. Just before serving, add sparkling water or ginger ale. Garnish with twists of fresh lemon, lime, and orange peel, if desired.

Makes about 42 servings.

SAN JOAQUIN EGGNOG

1 cup California port, red or white
1 cup water
**⅓ cup (about ½ of a 6-oz can)
frozen pineapple juice
concentrate, undiluted**
¼ teaspoon salt
¼ teaspoon powdered allspice
1 quart eggnog

Combine all ingredients but eggnog; then beat slowly into eggnog.

Makes about 17 servings.

Good wine carrieth a man to heaven.

PORT NOG

2 cups California port, chilled
1 (6 oz) can frozen pineapple juice
  concentrate, thawed
2 cups cold water
½ teaspoon powdered allspice
2 quarts eggnog
Ice block
Nutmeg

Place all ingredients except ice and nutmeg in punch bowl. Beat slowly until all ingredients are blended. Add ice. Stir. Sprinkle nutmeg over punch. Serve.

Makes about 24 servings.

PORT CREAM NOG

2 cups California port
½ cup California brandy
8 eggs, separated
1 teaspoon nutmeg
½ teaspoon cinnamon
½ cup sugar
1 quart vanilla ice cream, melted
1 quart milk

Place egg yolks in large mixing bowl. Beat egg yolks. Beat in nutmeg, cinnamon and sugar. Beat in brandy and port. Stir in ice cream and milk. In separate bowl beat egg whites until stiff. Blend egg whites into egg yolk mixture. Cover and chill overnight. Transfer to chilled punch bowl when ready to serve. Stir and serve.

Makes about 22 servings.

Hot Drinks

HOLIDAY GLOGG

6 dried figs
1 cup whole almonds, blanched
1½ cups raisins
10 whole cardamoms, cracked
6 whole cloves
2 cinnamon sticks
Peel from 3 oranges, cut in strips
2 (750 ml) bottles California white
   dinner wine
1 (750 ml) bottle California red
   dinner wine
½ cup sugar

Combine figs, almonds, raisins, cardamom, cloves, cinnamon, orange, and one
bottle of white wine in large saucepan or
pot. Cover and heat. Do not boil. Remove from heat and set aside for two
days. When ready to serve, remove fruits
and spices. Add one bottle white wine
and red wine. Stir in sugar. Heat to simmer. Do not boil. Serve in preheated
mugs with raisins and almonds in each
mug.

Makes about 20 servings.

For when we quaff the gen'rous bowl,
Then sleep the sorrows of our soul.

CINNAMON SHERRY TODDY

1 quart eggnog
1 cup California sherry
¼ teaspoon cinnamon
1 cup milk
½ teaspoon salt
1 egg white
Cinnamon sticks

Mix eggnog, sherry and powdered cinnamon; beat well. Stir in milk and salt; heat gently to below boiling. Beat egg white to soft peaks; fold into hot nog. Serve with cinnamon sticks for stirring.

Makes about 16 servings.

WASSAIL BOWLE

For a holiday party, a Wassail Bowle is a grand and glorious old custom. Bake 6 apples, cored and filled with sugar. (Peel down 1-inch from top.) Meanwhile, in double boiler, heat 2 large bottles Tokay, sherry, or muscatel, with ½ teaspoon each nutmeg and cinnamon, 3 cloves, ½ cup sugar and 1 tablespoon grated lemon rind. Beat 4 egg yolks and whites separately until whites are stiff; fold together. Add hot wine slowly; beat until frothy. Put baked apples in bowl and pour hot liquid over. The name *wassail* comes from a cheery salute that went with the ancient drink in Northern Europe. Some recipes include ale along with the wine.

Makes about 12 servings.

BERKELEY SHERRY

2 cups California sherry
1 stick cinnamon
¼ cup sugar
¼ cup lemon juice
Lemon slices
Extra cinnamon sticks

Heat sherry with 1 stick cinnamon and sugar, just to boiling. Add lemon juice and pour into preheated cups. Add thin slice of lemon to each cup, with cinnamon stick for stirring.

Makes about 5 or 6 servings.

GLOG A LA MARION

¾ cup sugar
Dash of bitters
2 cups California red dinner wine
2 cups California sherry
1 cup California brandy
Raisins and unsalted almonds

Heat until piping hot. Place 1 large raisin and 1 almond in each preheated mug or cup and pour in Glog.

Makes about 13 servings.

Moderation in the drinking of good wine often is conducive to health and happiness. Wine-drinking peoples are never—or seldom—intemperate.

HOT SHERRY NOG

Beat 3 eggs and ¾ cup powdered sugar together until very thick. Heat 5 cups cream sherry and 2½ cups boiling water to simmering; do not boil. Preheat mugs or cups with boiling water. Place 3 tablespoons of egg-sugar batter in each mug or cup; add ¾ cup heated sherry mixture. Stir well and sprinkle with nutmeg. Serve at once.

Makes about 10 servings.

MULLED SHERRY

**1 (3 oz) package sweetened
    lemonade mix**
**1 cup orange-flavored instant
    breakfast drink**
½ teaspoon cinnamon
½ teaspoon cloves
California Sherry

Combine lemonade mix, orange-flavored breakfast drink, cinnamon and cloves; mix well. Store in airtight container. When ready to serve, spoon 1 tablespoon of the dry mixture into a heatproof mug or glass. Heat sherry to simmering. Pour desired amount into each mug; stir to blend flavors.

Makes about 12 servings.

HOT BUTTERED NOG

1 quart eggnog
1 cup milk
1 cup California sweet vermouth
¼ teaspoon salt
½ teaspoon ground coriander
Soft butter

Combine eggnog and milk; slowly beat in sweet vermouth. Stir in salt and coriander; heat gently to just below boiling. Pour into preheated cups or mugs and top each with ½ teaspoon soft butter.

Makes about 16 servings.

PORT WINE NEGUS

Port Wine Negus also goes back many generations. For about 11 servings (3 oz), put the juice of 1 lemon and the pared lemon rind in top of double boiler, with 2 tablespoons sugar. Pour in 1 large bottle (4 cups) port; heat just below boiling. Stir in 1 cup boiling water. Strain into preheated mugs or cups, and dust with nutmeg.

When wine enlivens the heart
May friendship surround the table.

HOT BUTTERED WINE

1 (6 oz) can frozen orange juice concentrate
2 cups water
2 cups California muscatel
⅛ teaspoon cinnamon
⅛ teaspoon nutmeg
½ cup sugar
1 tablespoon butter
½ fresh lemon, sliced

Combine all ingredients in saucepan or chafing dish and stir until sugar dissolves. Heat steaming hot, but do not boil. Serve at once.

Makes about 8 servings.

An electric slow-cooker pot, with controlled heat, is an excellent server for hot wine drinks, especially for large groups. Set heat regulator for simmering temperature, never boiling.

GLUH WEIN

Another traditional warmer, and great. In one cup, place a cinnamon stick, 2 dashes ground cinnamon, 4 whole cloves, 1 slice lemon peel (and 1 slice orange peel if desired) and ½ teaspoon sugar. Fill up cup with red dinner wine, well heated but not boiled.

BISHOP'S WINE

1 orange
Whole cloves
1 (3-inch) stick cinnamon
1 (750 ml) bottle California red
  dinner wine
½ cup sugar

Stud whole orange with cloves and heat in wine, with cinnamon, about ½ hour. Do not boil. Stir in sugar. Serve at once or keep hot in a double boiler. Marvelous aroma and flavor!

Another version of this very old recipe calls for oven-roasting or broiling the clove-stuck whole orange until soft and brown, then cutting into quarters before adding it to the hot wine. Port may also be used.

Makes about 8 servings.

MULLED RED

1½ cups California port
1 (750 ml) bottle California red
  dinner wine
½ cup sugar
¼ cup lemon juice
1 tablespoon cinnamon
¼ teaspoon nutmeg
½ teaspoon ground cloves
Lemon slices

Place all ingredients except lemon slices in top of double boiler. Heat for 30 minutes. Stir occasionally. Place lemon slice in each preheated mug. Serve.

Makes about 10 servings.

SWEDISH GLOG

¾ cup light or dark raisins
1 tablespoon whole cardamom
2 teaspoons whole cloves
3-inch stick cinnamon
1½ cups water
1 (750 ml) bottle California red
   dinner wine
½ cup sugar
¼ cup blanched almonds

Rinse and drain raisins; peel and crush cardamom, using mortar and pestle or sturdy knife. Combine spices, ½ cup of raisins and water, simmer ½ hour. Strain and add liquid to wine; stir in sugar and heat to simmering. Serve hot, with almonds and raisins in each cup.

Makes about 12 servings.

SCOTT'S WINE TORCH

3 cups apple juice
20 whole cloves
4 sticks cinnamon
Peel of 1 lemon, cut in strips
Juice of 1 lemon
1 (750 ml) bottle California red
   dinner wine
1 (750 ml) bottle California port
½ cup California brandy

Simmer apple juice, cloves, cinnamon, and lemon peel 15 minutes. Strain; add lemon juice, red dinner wine, and port; simmer again. Heat brandy, ignite it and ladle slowly into hot wine. Serve in preheated mugs, cups or glasses.

Makes about 25 servings.

HOT SPICED WINE

1 cup sugar
4 cups water
Spiral peel from half a lemon
18 whole cloves
2 (3-inch) stick cinnamon
2 (750 ml) bottles California red
  dinner wine

Dissolve sugar in water in large saucepan. Add slices of lemon peel, cloves, and cinnamon. Boil 15 minutes; then strain out peel and spices. Add wine and heat gently. Do not boil. Meanwhile, preheat the punch bowl or serving decanter by filling it with warm, then hot, water. When ready to serve, empty water from container and dry it. Pour in the mulled wine and serve immediately.

To make individual servings: Prepare recipe without the wine and store the spicy syrup in the refrigerator in a tightly covered container. For each drink, preheat mug or glass by rinsing with very hot water. Use 2 oz spiced syrup and 5 oz of wine. Heat just to simmering, and pour into preheated mug.

Makes about 20 servings.

Medieval German . . .

> Drink wine, and you will sleep well. Sleep well and you will not sin. Avoid sin, and you will be saved. Ergo, drink wine and be saved.

DANISH GLOGG

4 cinnamon sticks
24 whole cloves
1 cup California white dinner wine
1 cup slivered almonds
½ cup raisins
1 cup currants
¼ cup sugar
2 cups aquavit
1 (750 ml) bottle California port
2 (750 ml) bottles California red
   dinner wine
Orange slices

Place cinnamon, cloves, and white wine in saucepan. Cover. Bring to a boil. Reduce heat and simmer 45 minutes. Strain into large pot. Add remaining ingredients (except orange slices). Heat slowly. Do not boil. Preheat punch bowl. Pour mixture into punch bowl. Add orange slices. Serve in preheated mugs.

Makes about 28 servings.

MENDOCINO TREAT

12 eggs, separated
3 cups water
2 (750 ml) bottles California red
   dinner wine
Nutmeg

Beat egg whites and yolks in separate bowls. Pour water and wine in large saucepan and bring to simmer. Slowly stir in egg yolks and whites. Continue to simmer and stir until hot. Serve in preheated mugs. Sprinkle with nutmeg.

Makes about 20 servings.

JERRY'S SKI CUP

Rind of 1 lemon, cut in strips
¼ teaspoon cinnamon
8 whole cloves
½ cup sugar
2 cups California white dinner wine
2 lemon slices
½ teaspoon nutmeg
2 (750 ml) bottles California red
dinner wine
¼ cup California brandy

Place lemon rind, cinnamon, cloves, sugar, and white wine in large saucepan. Bring to a boil. Lower heat and simmer 30 minutes. Add remaining ingredients. Simmer and stir until hot. Strain and serve in preheated mugs.

Makes about 18 servings.

AFTER-SKI BOWL

12 very small apples
4 tablespoons white corn syrup
¼ cup sugar
½ teaspoon cinnamon
3 cups California white dinner wine
1½ cup apple cider
¼ teaspoon nutmeg
1 twist lemon peel

Roll apples in corn syrup to coat them in mixed sugar and cinnamon; bake in hot oven (400°F) 15 minutes. Meanwhile, mix remaining ingredients and heat slowly at least 15 minutes. Serve in wide mugs, preheated, an apple in each mug.

Makes about 12 servings.

ALPINE GLOGG

2 tablespoons bitters
3 cups raisins
2 cinnamon sticks
1 (2-inch) piece of whole ginger
12 whole cardamoms, crushed
12 whole cloves
Rind of 1 orange
2 cups California sherry
2 (750 ml) bottles California port
**2 (750 ml) bottles California red
  dinner wine**
1½ cups sugar
1½ cups aquavit
2 cups whole almonds

Place all ingredients except sugar, aquavit, and almonds in large enamel or stainless steel pot. Cover. Set aside for one day. When ready to serve, add sugar and aquavit. Stir. Allow to simmer until very hot. Add almonds. Serve hot in pre-heated mugs with nuts and raisins in each mug.

Makes about 42 servings.

MIDNIGHT TEA

A wonderful nightcap. For 16 servings, cover 1 tablespoon tea leaves with 3 cups boiling water. Steep 5 minutes, strain. Add ½ cup orange marmalade. Bring to boil; simmer 10 minutes; strain again. Add 1 large bottle white dinner wine, 2 tablespoons lemon juice, sugar to taste. Simmer again. Put thin lemon slice in each cup.

CHILL KILLER

2 egg yolks
1 tablespoon sugar
¼ cup coffee liqueur
1 cup California red dinner wine
Lemon slices
Nutmeg

Combine egg yolks, sugar, liqueur, and wine in saucepan. Stir constantly. Serve in preheated mugs. Add lemon slice in each mug and sprinkle with nutmeg.

Makes 2 servings.

MULLED CUP

1 (6 oz) can frozen pineapple juice
concentrate
¾ cup California white dinner wine
2½ cups water
⅛ teaspoon ground cloves
⅛ teaspoon ground allspice
Dash of salt
1 tablespoon sugar

Combine and heat slowly to just below boiling. Serve hot in preheated cups.

Makes about 10 servings.

Wine is the drink of the gods, milk the drink of babies, tea the drink of women, and water the drink of beasts.

BLACKBERRY WARMER

Rind of 1 lemon, grated
Juice of 1 lemon
2 whole cloves
1 teaspoon ground ginger
2 cups water
**4 cups California white dinner wine,
  hot**
1½ cups blackberry brandy

Place lemon rind, juice, cloves, ginger, and water in large saucepan. Bring to a boil. Simmer five minutes. Stir in hot wine and brandy. Serve hot in preheated mugs.

Makes about 16 servings.

LONDON NITEY

3 cups double strength tea
½ cup orange marmalade
2 tablespoons lemon juice
**1 (750 ml) bottle California white
  dinner wine**
Sugar to taste
Lemon slices

Combine tea and marmalade in saucepan. Simmer for ten minutes. Add lemon juice, wine, and sugar to taste. Heat. Do not boil. Pour in preheated mugs. Add lemon slice to each mug.

Makes about 8 servings.

BARBARA'S HOT TODDY

1 magnum California white dinner wine
1 tablespoon sugar
3 eggs
3 cups brandy

Heat wine in large saucepan. Do not boil. Add sugar and nutmeg. Remove from heat. Whip eggs. Slowly beat eggs into hot wine. Do not allow mixture to curdle. Beat in brandy. Serve in preheated mugs.

Makes about 20 servings.

ORANGE WINTER PUNCH

12 whole cloves
1 large orange, unpeeled
1 tablespoon sugar
1 (4/5-qt.) bottle California white table wine or Champagne
3 ounces California Brandy

Stick cloves into orange. Roast orange over an open fire until light brown. Cut orange into slices; place in saucepan. Add sugar; warm for an instant. Add wine and Brandy. Serve in preheated cups. Serves 8.

Nothing equals the joy of the drinker except the joy of the wine in being drunk.

BISHOP'S WINE

1 orange
Whole cloves
1 (3-inch) stick cinnamon
1 large bottle California Zinfandel
½ cup sugar

Stud whole orange with cloves and heat
in wine, with cinnamon, about ½ hour.
Do not boil. Stir in sugar. Serve at once,
or keep hot in a double boiler. Marvelous
aroma and flavor! (Note: Another version
of this very old recipe calls for oven-
roasting or broiling the clove-stuck whole
orange until soft and brown, then cutting
into quarters before adding it to the hot
wine. California Port may also be used.)

About 8 servings

WINTER WARM-UP

Just the thing to warm the hearts of those
coming in from the cold. California
Sherry or Muscatel joins with orange
juice to make this special hot mug.

1 (4/5-qt.) bottle California Sherry or
** Muscatel**
6 cups orange juice
1 teaspoon ground cardamom

In saucepan heat all ingredients to simmering. Remove from heat and pour into
heat-proof mugs or glasses.

(12 4-oz. servings)

HOT WINE CRANBERRY CUP

For a speedy serving of a hot drink, prepare the special, spiced cranberry syrup ahead and store it in the refrigerator. It takes only a moment to combine it with California Burgundy or Claret to make this stimulating drink.

2 (1-pt.) bottles cranberry juice cocktail
2 cups water
1½ cups sugar
4 inches stick cinnamon
12 whole cloves
Peel ½ lemon
2 (4/5-qt.) bottles California Burgundy or Claret
¼ cup lemon juice

Combine all ingredients but wine and lemon juice in saucepan; bring to boil, stirring until sugar is dissolved. Simmer gently 15 minutes, then strain. Combine syrup with wine and lemon juice; heat, but do not boil. Serve in preheated mugs or cups; serve with a sprinkling of nutmeg.

(About 28 3-oz. servings)

> For of all labors, none transcend
> The works that on the brain depend;
> Nor could we finish great designs
> Without the pow'r of gen'rous wines.

CALIFORNIA CAUDLE

This makes a good drink for the holidays.

6 egg yolks
4 cups California Muscatel or other dessert wine
6 cups strong black tea
1 cup sugar
Grated nutmeg

Beat egg yolks until light and lemon colored. Add wine and tea; beat with rotary beater. Add sugar. Heat in double boiler. Serve in heated mugs topped with a sprinkling of grated nutmeg.

NOTE: *Caudles were popular in 17th century England, when they were served in small two-handled silver cups as a warming refreshment. They are just as delicious today, as an around-the-fire drink.*

(12 to 20 servings)

HOT LEMON SWIZZLE EGGNOG

1 quart commercial eggnog
1 cup milk
1 cup California Muscatel or Sherry
¼ teaspoon salt
2 teaspoons grated lemon rind
Nutmeg
Curls of lemon peel

Combine eggnog and milk. Slowly beat in Muscatel. Stir in salt and lemon rind. Heat gently to just below boiling. Top each serving with a dash of nutmeg and a lemon peel curl.

(About 16 servings, 3-oz. size)

About the Author . . .

California Wine Drinks is Master Knight of the Vine, William I. Kaufman's 142nd published book. As a photographer he has had 17 one-man shows. Known also as the world's most published cookbook writer for his 90 books on the subject of food. For many years his lecture tours brought cooking ideas to Woman's Clubs throughout America. His International Party Series has sold millions of copies. In the field of wine, he wrote *The Pocket Encyclopedia of California Wine* and received the prestigous *GOLD VINE AWARD* for bringing practical information to the American consumer. His other wine books include: the splendid gift book (illustrated) *Champagne, the Whole World Wine Catalog* and *The Travellers Guide to the Vineyards of North America.* In many cases such as *Perfume* and *Champagne* he illustrated the book himself. Published by every major publisher in the world, space does not allow us to include all the multi-careers of this truly renaissance man.

Index

WINE APPRECIATION GUILD ORDER FORM—1377 Ninth Avenue, San Francisco, California 94122

SHIP TO: _____

Address _____

City _____ State _____ Zip _____

____ Copies #500 EPICUREAN RECIPES OF CALIFORNIA WINEMAKERS		$5.95@
____ Copies #501 GOURMET WINE COOKING THE EASY WAY		$5.95@
____ Copies #502 NEW ADVENTURES IN WINE COOKERY		$5.95@
____ Copies #503 FAVORITE RECIPES OF CALIFORNIA WINEMAKERS		$5.95@
____ Copies #504 WINE COOKBOOK OF DINNER MENUS		$5.95@
____ Copies #505 EASY RECIPES OF CALIFORNIA WINEMAKERS		$5.95@
____ Copies #640 THE CHAMPAGNE COOKBOOK		$5.95@
____ Copies #527 IN CELEBRATION OF WINE & LIFE		$9.95@
____ Copies #554 WINE CELLAR RECORD BOOK		$29.95@
____ Copies #641 POCKET ENCYCLOPEDIA OF CALIFORNIA WINES		$4.95@
____ Copies #671 CORKSCREWS		$12.95@
____ Copies #672 WINE IN EVERYDAY COOKING		$5.95@
____ Copies #673 CALIFORNIA WINE DRINK BOOK		$4.95@
____ Copies #721 CALIFORNIA BRANDY DRINK BOOK		$4.95@

California Residents 6% sales tax _____

Plus $1.50 Shipping and handling (per order) $1.50

TOTAL enclosed or charged to credit card _____

Charge to Mastercard or Visa card # _____

Expiration Date _____

Signature _____